THOMAS KINKADE
The Voice of Creation

HARVEST HOUSE™ PUBLISHERS

EUGENE, OREGON

The Voice of Creation

Text Copyright © 2002 by Media Arts Group, Inc., Morgan Hill, CA 95037
and Harvest House Publishers, Eugene, OR 97402
Published by Harvest House Publishers, Eugene, OR 97402

Library of Congress Cataloging-in-Publication Data

Kinkade, Thomas, 1958-
    The voice of creation / Thomas Kinkade.
      p. cm.
    ISBN 0-7369-0781-5
    1. Kinkade, Thomas, 1958- 2. Plein air painting—United States. 3.
Creation (Literary, artistic, etc.) I. Title.
    ND237.K535 A4 2002
    759.13—dc21   2002001517

Text for this book has been excerpted from *Simpler Times* by Thomas Kinkade (Harvest House Publishers, 1996).

All works of art reproduced in this book are copyrighted by Thomas Kinkade and may not be copied or reproduced
without the artist's permission. For information regarding Thomas Kinkade art prints, collectibles, and other products,
please contact:

    Media Arts Group, Inc.
    900 Lightpost Way
    Morgan Hill, CA 95037
    1-800-366-3733

Design and Production by Koechel Peterson & Associates, Minneapolis, Minnesota

Scripture quotations are from the Holy Bible: New International Version®. NIV®. Copyright © 1973, 1978, 1984
by the International Bible Society. Used by permission of Zondervan Publishing House.

Harvest House Publishers has made every effort to trace the ownership of all poems and quotes. In the event of a
question arising from the use of a poem or quote, we regret any error made and will be pleased to make the necessary
correction in future editions of this book.

Printed in Hong Kong

02 03 04 05 06 07 08 09 10 11 / NG / 10 9 8 7 6 5 4 3 2 1

The loudest message the natural world

speaks to me has always been a

comforting, uplifting message about God

and His connection with my world.

THOMAS KINKADE

I believe in the brook as it wanders

From hillside into glade;

I believe in the breeze as it whispers

When evening's shadows fade.

I believe in the roar of the river

As it dashes from high cascade;

I believe in the cry of the tempest

'Mid the thunder's cannonade.

I believe in the light of shining stars,

I believe in the sun and the moon;

I believe in the flash of lightning,

I believe in the night-bird's croon.

I believe in the faith of the flowers,

I believe in the rock and sod,

For in all of these appeareth clear

The handiwork of God.

Author Unknown

Stones and trees speak slowly and may take a week to get out a single sentence, and there are few men, unfortunately, with the patience to wait for an oak to finish a thought.

—Garrison Keillor

There's a little beach town

not far from our home where our family loves to go for weekends. I set up my portable easel and paint in the brisk, salty air. The girls play in the sand. We all take walks on the shore. It's a great opportunity to be out-of-doors and to get away from it all.

But one of my favorite things to do when we're down at the beach is watch the people. I like to sit on the little patio with a cup of coffee and just enjoy the human parade on the scenic walk below.

It is not the language of painters but the language of nature which one should listen to...The feeling for the things themselves, for reality, is more important than the feeling for pictures.

—Vincent van Gogh

I'm especially fascinated

by all the different things people do there on the edge of the ocean while the sun is smiling and the waves are caressing the shore.

Some walk by in twos, deeply engaged in conversation.

Some pound the sand with their running shoes as they stride along, their faces deep in athletic concentration.

MY HEART IS AWED *within me when I think*

Of the great miracle that still goes on,

In silence, round me—the perpetual work

Of thy creation, finished, yet renewed

Forever. Written on thy works I read

The lesson of thy own eternity.

—*William Cullen Bryant*

My heart is awed

If one looks long enough at almost anything, looks with absolute attention at a flower, a stone, the bark of a tree, grass, snow, a cloud, something like revelation takes place.

—May Sarton

Skaters weave in and out

among the foot traffic on the paved path with barely a glance at the bicyclers and the stroller pushers and the tourists with their cameras and the readers in their beach chairs. Children are everywhere, their high-pitched voices mingling with the sound of seagulls and surf.

But who can paint like Nature?

Can imagination boast,

amid its gay creation, hues like hers?

—James Thomson

Every once in a while,

someone will come out to the beach and sit motionless on a rock. Maybe they intend to stay for just a few minutes. But those few minutes quickly become an hour, and before long they've grown entranced by the rhythms of the surf. Hour after hour they sit patiently near the ocean, studying it and listening to its voice. They may be there until sunset with nothing to show for their day but a sunburn and a peaceful heart.

And those are the people, I suspect, who hear the voice of creation.

I said it for the first time

AS IF FOR THE FIRST TIME, *indeed, creation noiselessly sank into*

and through me its placid and untellable

lesson, beyond— O, so infinitely beyond!—

anything from art, books, sermons, or from science, old or new. The

spirit's hour—religion's hour—the visible suggestion of God in space

and time—now once definitely indicated, if never again.

—*Walt Whitman*

And this our life...

Finds tongues in trees, books in the running brooks,

Sermons in stones, and good in everything.

—William Shakespeare

It's no secret

that human beings can find healing and restoration through contact with nature. It's no secret that growing things soothe the mind, that wild things uplift the soul, that rocks and hills and trees do something undefinable but positive for the human spirit.

May the glory of the LORD endure forever;

May the LORD rejoice in his works.

—The Book of Psalms

Something deep in our spirit

makes us long to be out-of-doors, to be renewed by the

presence of nature. If you listen, the world of sky and water

and trees can teach you. It can change you. It can make

your life profoundly simpler and more satisfying.

But you have to be paying attention. You have to be

still. You have to listen and touch and smell. And

sometimes you have to wait.

TO THE BODY AND MIND *which have been cramped by*

noxious work or company, nature is medicinal and

restores their tone. The tradesman, the attorney comes

out of the din and craft of the street and sees

the sky and the woods, and is a man again. In their eternal

calm, he finds himself. The health of the eye seems to demand

a horizon. We are never tired, so long as we can see far enough.

—*Ralph Waldo Emerson*

Body and mind

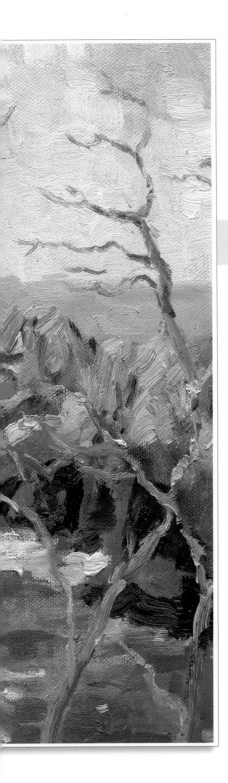

> *The beautiful is in nature, and it is encountered under the most diverse forms of reality. Once it is found it belongs to art, or rather to the artist who discovers it.*
>
> —*Gustave Courbet*

I am not by nature

a quiet or reflective type. It was my pencils and paints that taught me to listen to nature rather than just visit nature. It was my art that slowed me down enough to see and hear the stories of the natural world.

From the time I was very small, I carried a sketchbook with me when I went on a hike or a long bike ride. I loved to loll on the golden hillsides and sketch the lumpy green oak trees or the patterns of the clouds.

Must be out-of-doors enough to get experience of wholesome reality, as a ballast to thought and sentiment. Health requires this relaxation, this aimless life.

—*Henry David Thoreau*

As I grew a little older,

I took my paints outdoors as well. I began the practice of plein-air painting—which simply means painting on location, out-of-doors. I started with just a few brushes and a jar of turpentine and a couple of tubes of paint packed away in a satchel. Today I use a portable studio I designed myself—a lightweight box that holds my paints and canvas, and folds up into an easel. I can even attach a little umbrella to protect me from sun and rain.

Thomas Kinkade

WHEN I CONSIDER *your heavens,*

the work of your fingers,

the moon and the stars,

which you have set in place,

what is man that you are mindful of him,

the son of man that you care for him?

— *The Book of Psalms*

There is nothing that God hath established in a constant course of nature, and which therefore is done every day, but would seem a Miracle, and exercise our admiration, if it were done but once.

—John Donne

I can take my portable studio

almost anywhere my feet can walk. I have taken it to the desert, to the mountains, to New England villages and Irish castles, to the streets of Paris and San Francisco. I've even set it up in my own backyard and painted while the children played around me and attempted a few dabs with the paints themselves.

There is a pleasure

THERE IS A PLEASURE *in the pathless woods,*

There is a rapture on the lonely shore,

There is society where none intrudes

By the deep sea, and music in its roar.

———————————————————————————

— *George Gordon*

Time to put off the world and go somewhere
And find my health again in the search.

—W. B. Yeats

Plein-air painting

gives me an excuse to get outdoors. It gives me

backgrounds and ideas for my paintings. But most

important, it forces me to experience nature on its own

terms. When I am painting a scene, I'm not just walking

through it or skating through it or skiing down it. I am

sitting still for hours at a time, soaking it in, observing

the details, breathing in the air, and listening to the

sounds. I am becoming a part of the natural world and

letting it become a part of me.

HE ALONE STRETCHES OUT *the heavens*

and treads on the waves of the sea. He is the

Maker of the Bear and Orion, the Pleiades and

the constellations of the south. He performs

wonders that cannot be fathomed, miracles that

cannot be counted.

—*The Book of Job*

He alone stretches out

God dreamed—the suns sprang flaming into place,

And sailing worlds with many a venturous race.

He woke—His smile alone illumined space.

—Ambrose Bierce

But you don't have to

be a painter to have this same experience. You can be a

bird watcher. You can take a journal to a little park behind

your house. You can take a walk in the woods or a drive

out to a desert spring.

The point is to be quiet and receptive.

The point is to watch and listen for nature's messages.

This is the meeting place

THIS IS THE MEETING PLACE *where God has set his*

bounds. Here is enough, at last, for eye and

thought, restful and satisfying and illimitable. Here rest

is sweet, and the picture of it goes with us on our homeward

way, more lasting in memory than the sunset on the

meadows or the lingering light across the silent stream.

—Isaac Ogden Rankin

I hear beyond the range of sound,

I see beyond the range of sight,

New earths and skies and seas around,

And in my day the sun doth pale his light.

—*Henry David Thoreau*

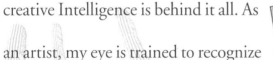To me, the beauty and intricacy

and magnificence of the outside world have always

shouted the unmistakable message that an astoundingly

creative Intelligence is behind it all. As

an artist, my eye is trained to recognize

work. And the work I see in a fiery fluorescent autumn

tree or in craggy tumbled boulders or the subtle

patchwork of color in a sun-kissed field bespeaks an

imagination and a craftsmanship far beyond that of

any human artist.

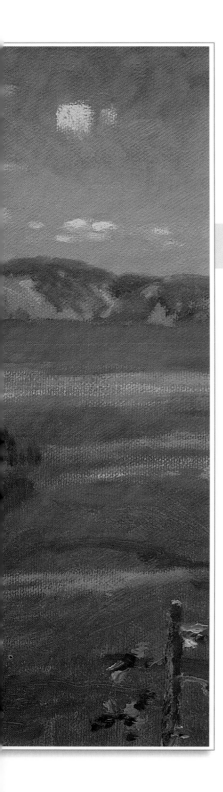

Earth has not anything to show more fair:
Dull would he be of soul who could pass by
A sight so touching in its majesty!
—*William Wordsworth*

The loudest message

the natural world speaks to me has always been a

comforting, uplifting message about God and His

connection with my world.

But you don't have to take my word for it.

Listen to the trees, to what they have to say to you.

Listen to the ocean, to the many-voiced stories the

waves tell.

Listen to the sun, the moon, the stars; to the echoing,

intimate voice of the heavens.

THE HEAVENS DECLARE *the glory of God;*

the skies proclaim the work of his hands.

Day after day they pour forth speech;

night after night they display knowledge.

There is no speech or language

where their voice is not heard.

Their voice goes out into all the earth,

their words to the ends of the world.

—*The Book of Psalms*

The heavens declare

List of Paintings